Fear,
Get Thee
Behind Me

Overcoming the Mental
Warfare of Fear

Fear, Get Thee Behind Me

Overcoming the Mental Warfare of Fear

Aesha R. Minter

Fear, Get Thee Behind Me

© 2015, Aesha R. Minter

Basar Publishing

ISBN: **978-1-942013-78-5**

Printed in the United States of America

Editors: Tiffany Buckner, Stephanie Chapman

Cover Design: Tiffany Buckner

Photography: Jermaine Johnson

Dedications

To my Lord and Savior, Jesus Christ, who has anointed me to complete my first literary work: Lord, I present this manuscript to you.

To my mother, Pamela L. Minter, who encourages me to always pursue my dreams: I love you, Ma.

To my Beloved Aunt (the late Valerie Johnson), a creative writer and poet: I miss you dearly.

To Ameenah, Joy and Bria for your special contributions: Much love to you ladies :)

To my City **#OneBaltimore** as we strive to promote peace in our community.

Acknowledgments

First, I would like to give kudos to Apostle Charles Smith Jr., who is the founder of Kingdom Nation International Ministries, Inc.

I met this awesome man of God in 2008 at a dance conference in Florida. Thanks for seeing the writing gift in me before I knew I had it, and thank you for releasing a prophetic Word into my life about the books that were coming forth through me.

I am also grateful for my book writing coaches Pastor Rekesha Pittman (founder of the Eagle Authors Training Institute) and Tiffany Buckner, my instructor for the Remnant Writers course and founder of Anointed Fire. These women are the spiritual midwives who taught me how to strategically birth this book into the marketplace.

In addition, I acknowledge my friend and mentor, Lady Paulette Rolle-Alesnik, who is a powerful international dancer, author, prayer warrior and conference speaker.

Preface

While I was writing this manuscript, I encountered many challenges that caused me to doubt whether I'd be able to release this book. On Monday, April 28, 2015, the city of Baltimore (my place of residence) was shut down due to civil unrest and protests against police brutality. This was sparked by the murder of a young black man by the name of Freddie Gray. Over the two weeks that followed, my city was under fire, crime rates spiked and my heart was grieving over the numerous murders that were occurring daily. A spirit of violence hovered over this area, and I was in prayer constantly because of the state of emergency that Baltimore was experiencing.

There were many other distractions during the course of writing this book that almost led me to abort this assignment. I was constantly having a conversation with fear. Negative thoughts incessantly flooded my mind.

In the midst of this mental battle, I decided to refute the fiery darts of my thoughts by declaring, "Fear, get thee behind me!" On the opposite side of fear, you will discover your true identity and embrace your calling in life.

Table of Contents

Introduction

I was inspired to write this book about fear because it is a common barrier that blocks growth, development and achievement. I know because overcoming fear was a personal struggle of mine until I decided to break free from mental bondage and fulfill the calling of God on my life. Throughout this book, I will cover the following elements: my definition of fear, the characteristics of fear and my personal testimony. I will also provide practical and spiritual steps to overcoming fear.

Every person has been presented

with opportunities to manifest greatness. What goals, visions and dreams have you placed on hold due to doubt and worry? When you operate out of fear, you fail to live and you do not thrive in your purpose for existing. God has given you the free will to rule, reign and have dominion over your circumstances.

My beloved reader, it is my desire that you will break free from the bondage of fear and everything that has prevented you from reaching your goals in life and manifesting your dreams. I understand the mental torment brought on by fear because I have wrestled with it myself. May the words written in the pages of this manuscript bring forth breakthrough and permanent change in your life and help you to walk boldly in your sphere of influence.

The following poem best summarizes the notion that fear is a power struggle between identity and destiny:

Our Deepest Fear ~ by Marianne Williamson

"Our deepest fear is not that we are inadequate. Our deepest fear is that we are powerful beyond measure. It is our light, not our darkness that most frightens us.

We ask ourselves, Who am I to be brilliant, gorgeous, talented, fabulous? Actually, who are you not to be? You are a child of God. Your playing small does not serve the world.

There is nothing enlightened about shrinking so that other people won't feel insecure around you. We are all meant to shine, as children do. We were born to make manifest the glory of God that is within us. It's not just in some of us; it's in everyone.

And as we let our own light shine, we unconsciously give other people permission to do the same. As we are liberated from our own fear, our presence automatically liberates others."

Chapter 1

Fear, the Silent Killer

Chapter 1
Fear, The Silent Killer

Darkness. Paralysis. Lethargy. Immobilization. Breathlessness. Numbness. Silence. Death. I am called Fear - The Silent Killer. I function like a disease that spreads rapidly through a deteriorating mind.

Let us examine the scripture in the book of Psalm 23:4*: "**Yea, though I walk through the valley of the shadow of death, I will fear no evil: for thou art**

3

with me; thy rod and staff comfort me."

In this passage, fear is defined as a "shadow of death" or an illusion to a certain reality. Think of fear as a death trap or death walk. The devil wants to scare you to the point where you become petrified and lie breathless without movement or progression.

Simon Peter was sought by the adversary to "sift as wheat", according to Luke 22:31. By definition, the word *sift* means to rip into shreds or pieces. Sifting is a violent motion that rapidly shifts an object back and forth across a sharp surface until it is shredded. Fear will place a person in darkness, confusion and mental torment. Intimidation is a fear tactic used by the enemy to cause you to draw back or digress.

PRAYER POINT

Lord, I declare that I am not driven by the shadow of darkness
through fear.
I allow the light of God's Word to shine brightly to drive out the enemy.

Chapter 2

The Fear Factor

Chapter 2
The Fear Factor

Fear must be conquered in order for a person to develop, grow and make progress in life. It influences our destinies, thoughts and actions. Apprehension hinders growth and frequently causes stress. This stress contributes to various ailments and diseases such as strokes, heart attacks, chest pains and skin outbreaks.

Fear creates mental blockages that may result in continuous cycles of failure. It is also a dream killer that reduces the momentum required to pursue success. Furthermore, it breaks the spirit, and this, in turn, prevents intimacy, oneness and commitment. Additionally, fear creates inferiority complexes and low self-esteem. Our self-esteem is essential to developing healthy relationships.

Fear is bondage of the mind, body and spirit. It is the opposite of faith. Faith is waiting to see the impossible happen when there is no evidence that it will happen. Fear is the antagonist of love and it breeds mistrust, disappointment and anxiety. It prevents the manifestation of dreams because our dreams are only manifested through our faith.

Fear is the greatest enemy of mankind. According to the *National Institute of Mental Health (NIMH)*, fear is a panic disorder that causes sudden and repeated mental attacks over a period of time. It is brought on by a person's need to control a situation. A person bound by fear feels the need to remain in control because of an illusion of unforeseen disaster or danger.

Universal studies have shown that fear triggers the fight-or-flight response. According to the *Encyclopedia Britannica*, the fight-or-flight response is a physiological response that affects the central nervous system or CNS. The fight-or-flight response was first described by Walter Bradford Cannon, and basically, it explains how an animal reacts to a perceived or real threat. The animal will either fight or flee.

Apprehension is also linked to other common anxiety disorders such as obsessive-compulsive disorder (OCD) and post-traumatic stress disorder. The severity of phobic responses cause trauma. Research conducted by The American Psychological Association (www.apa.org) showed that trauma is an emotional response to a mentally distressing event.

According to *Strong's Concordance* (5401), the Greek word for fear is "phobeo" (fob-eh'-o). It is interesting to note that fear has two Hebrew root words with significant differences in definition: (1) *pahhad* (terror or dread) and (2) *yarah* (reverence or respect).

God did not give us a spirit of fear, therefore, fear stems from Satan, himself. It is often provoked by our personal experiences of trauma, abuse, negative thought patterns and feeling powerless. There are three primary fears: (1) Fear of Self - creates feelings of inadequacy; causes inability to face your own character traits; form of sabotage. (2) Fear of People - avoiding people due to insecurities and false perceptions of self.

(3) <u>Fear of Risk</u> - avoiding situations, places and people because of doubt and uncertainty.

PRAYER POINT

Lord, I pull down every root of fear, self-doubt and unbelief. I declare that my physical body is subject to the peace of God and I supernaturally release healing and repel fear-based thoughts.

Chapter 3

Control Your
Thoughts

Chapter 3
Control Your Thoughts

Fear begins with negative thoughts. How many times have you become idle by sitting on the dreams God has placed within you? I am sure there have been times where you confessed with your mouth that you would reach your goals, but instead of taking the pain-staking steps towards fulfilling them, you froze with fear. This was because you thought those goals were unreachable or insurmountable based on past experiences and present insecurities.

Make up in your mind that you will no longer be bound by fear. Speak to fear, face it and annihilate it through the power of confession. Faith annihilates fear, and it is important not to abandon the Word of God because the Word builds faith.

Always remember that you have the power to control your thoughts and mind by casting down your fears. Thoughts control our actions. If we are not careful about guarding our minds, we will risk being overtaken by negative thought patterns. Ephesians 4:23 (KJV) says: "And be renewed in the spirit of your mind." It is my prayer that every mind attack from the enemy coming against you be demolished, canceled and rendered powerless in the name of Jesus! May the Lord God, the Prince of Peace, prevail in your heart and mind.

In Psalm 27:1-4, King David's mindset demonstrates fearlessness in the midst of his enemies:

> The LORD is my light and my salvation; whom shall I fear? the LORD is the strength of my life; of whom shall I be afraid? When the wicked, even mine enemies and my foes, came upon me to eat up my flesh, they stumbled and fell. Though an

host should encamp against me, my heart shall not fear: though war should rise against me, in this will I be confident. One thing have I desired of the LORD, that will I seek after; that I may dwell in the house of the LORD all the days of my life, to behold the beauty of the LORD, and to enquire in his temple.

No matter what you are facing today, know that Jesus will not allow trouble to overtake you. God promises to deliver you from every affliction when you rely on Him. The Lord is true to His Word. Don't you dare quit! Don't you dare allow depression to overtake your mind! The enemy cannot chase you with fears when you are in the presence of the Lord, for His presence brings eternal peace.

Control your thoughts also by examining your belief system. If you are constantly feeding your mind with doubt, worry, shame and pessimism, you will sabotage your ability to activate faith.

When you are in bondage to apprehension, then you are emotionally bound to the illusion of self. Just imagine what your life would be like if you didn't fear anything or anyone but God. How large would that business God has given you have grown if it had been launched ten years ago? Would you have been the next Olympic star, world-renowned surgeon or national television evangelist?

I urge you today not to feed your inner-man (spirit) with doubt and worry any longer. The authentic YOU cannot be revealed until you resist fear and act upon faith! Those who have great impacts in their spheres of influence are those who reject fear, all the while, focusing on the visions God has set before them.

How long will you allow the enemy to terrorize you through mind attacks? Push through the discomfort. Perhaps, it's time to birth that business you've been dreaming about. How long will you sit back year after year waiting for the perfect time to launch that big idea or vision? Your divine release has come to launch you out into the deep waters of imagination, innovation and inspiration.

PRAYER POINT

By the Spirit of God, I declare my thoughts are free from worry, doubt, anxiety and fear.

Chapter 4

Uncharted Territory

Chapter 4
Uncharted Territory

"Do not go where the path may lead,

go instead where there is no path

and leave a trail."

~ Ralph Waldo Emerson

There are many circumstances that
will often lead you to the crossroads of
some major decisions. During these
times of transition, you may experience
loneliness because you will begin to
evaluate: (1) where you are now, (2) who

you are now and (3) what you will become in the future. If not dealt with properly, this form of self-loathing can lead you to wandering throughout life without any sense of direction.

It is ultimately your responsibility to take a leap of faith and blaze trails by embracing the boldness that lies within you. The Bible says in 2 Timothy 1:7, "For God has not given us the spirit of fear; but of power, love and a sound mind." Regardless of the traumatic events you have been through in life, understand that your path has now been illuminated to bring purpose to your existence.

Many leaders in the marketplace

and ministry become influential because they were willing to take risks (despite their fears) to execute the visions, dreams and missions given to them by God. They were willing to go through uncharted territories and uncertainty because they had faith in God. They had to conquer the fear of the unknown to move forward. It is impossible to tap into the greatness within you if you are not willing to surrender your plans to the Lord so that He can perform His perfect will in your life.

Examine the character of Abraham in the Bible. According to Genesis 12:1-9, the Lord called Abraham (along with his wife Sarah) to move away from his residence (Haran) into the land of Canaan, and the Lord prophesied that he would be a father [blessing] to many nations. This calling came abruptly and without warning. Because of his faith in God, Abraham left a familiar place and embraced the fear of the unknown.

PRAYER POINT

I declare I am a trail-blazer. Lord, help me to fully embrace the fear of the unknown to walk in my God-ordained assignment.

Chapter 5

Speak to the Mountain

Chapter 5
Speak To The Mountain

"For assuredly, I say to you, whoever says to this mountain, 'Be removed and be cast into the sea, and does not doubt in his heart, but believes that those things he says will be done, he will have what-ever he says" ~ Mark 11:23.

Your path is already mapped out before you. You have gained new ground by walking in uncharted territory. Now, it is time to speak to every barrier and blockage placed in your life and tell it to be removed in the name of Jesus. Refuse to get discouraged about the challenges you are facing today. Just continue to break through until you reach your breakthrough. Go forth in spite of the distractions around you.

I challenge you to embark on a fearless journey, walk in uncharted territories and speak to every mountain along the way. This requires you to come outside of your comfort zone for the sake of accomplishing your God-given purpose.

As you travel along this path, you

will discover opportunities that will stretch you beyond your imagination. For example, I first heard the call to write a book several years ago when a prophetic word was spoken over me at a dance conference in Florida. Because of fear, I did not answer the call to write until November of 2014. The moment I made the decision to complete the work of becoming an author, I began a fearless journey to be all the Lord has called me to be. This breakthrough experience has changed my life forever, and it will also lead others to break free from their fears.

PRAYER POINT

Lord, I activate my faith and command every mountain in my life to be removed.

Chapter 6

Don't Wait

Chapter 6
Don't Wait

Time is accelerating, so be quick to move in your purpose. You must carry out your God-given assignment with boldness, urgency and unwavering faith. Flow with the Spirit of God and His grace will allow you to handle every challenge you face with ease.

Don't wait. Persevere! God's plans always require movement. The Lord is not moved by your declaration of faith only, but He requires your act of obedience. Procrastination is a result of fear and will keep you feeling lethargic and passive. Stop listening to the voice of the enemy telling you to slow down. Do you realize we are living in the last days? Jesus Christ will be returning soon. That business plan you have written for many years must be implemented NOW. Your call to public speaking must be activated because there are people who need to hear your voice in their communities. The world is waiting on you, but you must stop waiting on the world to validate your assignment for you. It is time to awaken the dream inside! Don't let it die because of fear and complacency. The time to act is now.

Answer the call on your life, move
forward in the Lord and push until
something happens.

PRAYER POINT

I declare that I will pursue my
dreams without hesitation.
Through the Lord's help, I will
reach my fullest potential
courageously.

Chapter 7

Forecast Your Future

Chapter 7
Forecast Your Future

You can create your own future by how you choose to live today. According to the *Oxford Dictionary*, forecasting is defined as the process of predicting or estimating a future event or trend. Likewise, we have the power to forecast our future by speaking positive things into our own lives before they happen. In the secular realm, this is known as a self-fulfilling prophecy.

It's going to happen! You have

been anointed, appointed and chosen for such a time as this. Go forth and take authority over your destiny. My beloved, please understand that you have the power to determine your own future. You have the power to change your environment. Shift the atmosphere by declaring for yourself what God has already spoken about you.

PRAYER POINT

I declare that my future is greater, and I do not fear success.
I possess the power to change my past by speaking into my future.

Chapter 8

Get Out of the Box

Chapter 8
Get Out of the Box

It is time to come out of your hiding place of obscurity. Come out of darkness! Come out of the shadows! The box represents boundaries, blockages and hindrances. In Psalm 23:4, the Bible says, "Yea, though I walk through the valley of the shadow of death, I will fear no evil: for thou art with me; thy rod and thy staff they comfort me." Understand that where you are now is not your final stop.

We live in a society that promotes

status quo. If you are among the minority with a different worldview than most, you will be rejected by the majority. Stepping out of the box (comfort zone) is the path to greatness.

PRAYER POINT

Lord, remove every blockage in my life that hinders movement and progression. I choose to push beyond my comfort zone to fulfill my purpose on the earth.

Chapter 9

Cross the Finish Line

Chapter 9
Cross The Finish Line

Complete what you started. The finish line is right in front of you. Faith requires that you act upon what appears impossible. Making excuses is just a cop-out. How long will you wrestle with your thoughts? In order to stop fear from overtaking you, you must learn to make a decision and run with it.

There is a universal saying that "an idle mind is the devil's playground."

Procrastination oftentimes lead to idleness and double-mindedness. The scripture says in James 1:8, "The double-minded man is unstable in all his ways." Instability leads further to indecision. All of these elements result from the spirit of fear.

PRAYER POINT

Lord, I declare that I am no longer bound by indecision. I will run with the vision or idea that God has given me with clarity.
I am a finisher!

Chapter 10

Embrace Change

Chapter 10
Embrace Change

According to the famous physicist, Albert Einstein, insanity is "doing the same thing over and over again and expecting different results." As many times as we have heard this quote, the majority of us have continued to live in fear and are rarely comfortable with change. Mediocrity is the norm and the status quo mentality keeps most people from tapping into their greatest potential in life. The late Dr. Myles Munroe, who was a world renowned motivational speaker, once stated or challenged all people to "die empty."

Mahatma Ghandi once said, "Be the change you want to see in the world."

Change is evident because life flows in seasons. As you become comfortable with change, you will grow in your ability to understand strategies that will help you effectively maneuver through the lifestyle that best suits you.

PRAYER POINT

I declare that I will make decisions wisely. I will run with the vision or idea that God has given me.
I am a finisher!

Chapter 11

Walk Fearlessly

Chapter 11
Walk Fearlessly

Steps to Conquer Fear

1. Make positive declarations about yourself daily.

2. Speak the Word of God over every fear until it is replaced by faith.

3. Meditate on the scriptures day and night.

4. Accept speaking engagements or enroll in a debate team or course.

5. Initiate conversations with strangers. This builds confidence and may cultivate the art of persuasion.

6. Enroll in a performing arts class to encourage freedom of expression. A

good class to enter, for example, is dance.

7. Pray aloud daily. It increases confidence in public speaking.

 8.Take classes related to your greatest passions, interests and gifting.

9. Speak positive affirmations daily.

10. Strive to live in peace.

11. Face your fears by engaging in conversations with the subject of fear.

12. Pay attention to your body and be calm.

13. Speak to every fear and command it to move.

Scriptures to Combat Fear

WAR AGAINST FEAR

Ephesians 6: 10-18

Finally, my brethren, be strong in the Lord, and in the power of his might. Put on the whole armor of God, that ye may be able to stand against the wiles of the devil. For we wrestle not against flesh and blood, but against principalities, against powers, against the rulers of the darkness of this world, against spiritual wickedness in high places. Wherefore take unto you the whole armor of God, that ye may be able to withstand in the evil day, and having done all, to stand. Stand therefore, having your loins girt about with truth, and having on the breastplate of righteousness. And your feet shod with the preparation of the gospel of peace. Above all, taking the shield of faith, wherewith ye shall be able to quench all the fiery darts of the wicked. And take the helmet of salvation, and the sword of the Spirit, which is the word of God. Praying always with all prayer and supplication in the Spirit, and watching thereunto with all perseverance and supplication for all saints.

PEACE DESTROYS FEAR

Jeremiah 29:11: "For I know the thoughts that I think toward you, says the Lord, thoughts of peace and not of evil, to give you an expected end."

Isaiah 26:3: "Thou wilt keep him in perfect peace, whose mind is stayed on thee: because he trusts in thee."

SPIRIT OF GOD OVERSHADOWS FEAR

2 Timothy 1:7: "For God has not given us the spirit of fear; but of power, love, and a sound mind."

Isaiah 41:10: "Fear not, for I am with you: be not dismayed; for I am your God: I will strengthen you; yea, I will help you; yeah, I will uphold you with the right hand of my righteousness."

LOVE REPELS FEAR

I John 4:18: "There is no fear in love; but perfect love casts out fear: because fear has torment. He that fears is not made perfect in love."

FAITH CONQUERS FEAR

Luke 1:37: "For with God nothing shall be impossible."

DELIVERANCE FROM FEAR

Psalm 34:4: "I sought the Lord, and he heard me, and delivered me from all my fears."

Psalm 23:4: "Yea, though I walk through the valley of the shadow of death, I will fear no evil: for thou art with me, thy rod and thy staff they comfort me."

ABOUT THE AUTHOR

Aesha R. Minter is an anointed visionary, author, change-agent and speaker. Her mission is to empower others to live fearlessly, promote marketplace ministry, and embrace a life of abundance. Ms. Minter is a Baltimore native who is a member of Empowerment Temple under the leadership of Pastor Dr. Jamal H. Bryant. She is also a graduate of the University of Maryland at College Park in the Nationally-Ranked Mathematics Program.

www.ingramcontent.com/pod-product-compliance
Lightning Source LLC
Chambersburg PA
CBHW062022040426

42447CB00010B/2101